DISCOVERING
SOUTH AMERICA
History, Politics, and Culture

GUYANA

DISCOVERING
SOUTH AMERICA
History, Politics, and Culture

GUYANA

Bob Temple

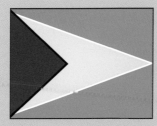

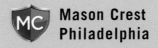

Mason Crest
Philadelphia

Mason Crest
450 Parkway Drive, Suite D
Broomall, PA 19008
www.masoncrest.com

Printed and bound in the United States of America.

CPSIA Compliance Information: Batch #DSA2015.
For further information, contact Mason Crest at 1-866-MCP-Book.

First printing
1 3 5 7 9 8 6 4 2

Library of Congress Cataloging-in-Publication Data
        on file at the Library of Congress

        ISBN: 978-1-4222-3300-9 (hc)
        ISBN: 978-1-4222-8643-2 (ebook)

Discovering South America: History, Politics, and Culture series ISBN: 978-1-4222-3293-4

DISCOVERING SOUTH AMERICA: History, Politics, and Culture

Argentina	Chile	Guyana	Suriname	South America:
Bolivia	Colombia	Paraguay	Uruguay	Facts & Figures
Brazil	Ecuador	Peru	Venezuela	

Table of Contents

KEY ICONS TO LOOK FOR:

Words to Understand: These words with their easy-to-understand definitions will increase the reader's understanding of the text, while building vocabulary skills.

Sidebars: This boxed material within the main text allows readers to build knowledge, gain insights, explore possibilities, and broaden their perspectives by weaving together additional information to provide realistic and holistic perspectives.

Research Projects: Readers are pointed toward areas of further inquiry connected to each chapter. Suggestions are provided for projects that encourage deeper research and analysis.

Text-Dependent Questions: These questions send the reader back to the text for more careful attention to the evidence presented there.

Series Glossary of Key Terms: This back-of-the book glossary contains terminology used throughout this series. Words found here increase the reader's ability to read and comprehend higher-level books and articles in this field.

Discovering South America

James D. Henderson

SOUTH AMERICA is a cornucopia of natural resources, a treasure house of ecological variety. It is also a continent of striking human diversity and geographic extremes. Yet in spite of that, most South Americans share a set of cultural similarities. Most of the continent's inhabitants are properly termed "Latin" Americans. This means that they speak a Romance language (one closely related to Latin), particularly Spanish or Portuguese. It means, too, that most practice Roman Catholicism and share the Mediterranean cultural patterns brought by the Spanish and Portuguese who settled the continent over five centuries ago.

Still, it is never hard to spot departures from these cultural norms. Bolivia, Peru, and Ecuador, for example, have significant Indian populations who speak their own languages and follow their own customs. In Paraguay the main Indian language, Guaraní, is accepted as official along with Spanish. Nor are all South Americans Catholics. Today Protestantism is making steady gains, while in Brazil many citizens practice African religions right along with Catholicism and Protestantism.

South America is a lightly populated continent, having just 6 percent of the world's people. It is also the world's most tropical continent, for a larger percentage of its land falls between the tropics of Cancer and Capricorn than is the case with any other continent. The world's driest desert is there, the Atacama in northern Chile, where no one has ever seen a drop of rain fall. And the world's wettest place is there too, the Chocó region of Colombia, along that country's border with Panama. There it rains almost every day. South America also has some of the world's highest mountains, the Andes,

Mountains and rivers along the Venezuela-Guyana border.

and its greatest river, the Amazon.

So welcome to South America! Through this colorfully illustrated series of books you will travel through 12 countries, from giant Brazil to small Suriname. On your way you will learn about the geography, the history, the economy, and the people of each one. Geared to the needs of teachers and students, each volume contains book and web sources for further study, a chronology, project and report ideas, and even recipes of tasty and easy-to-prepare dishes popular in the countries studied. Each volume describes the country's national holidays and the cities and towns where they are held. And each book is indexed.

You are embarking on a voyage of discovery that will take you to lands not so far away, but as interesting and exotic as any in the world.

(Opposite) An eroded peak near lakes in Guyana. (Right) Mighty Kaieteur Falls is five times the height of Niagara Falls and twice the height of Victoria Falls. It was named for a native chief, Kale, who according to legend paddled over the falls to appease the gods and save his tribe.

1 "Land of Waters"

THE NATION OF GUYANA (officially known as the Cooperative Republic of Guyana) received its name from the South American Indian word *guiana*, which means "land of waters." It's an apt description for this country, which not only borders the Atlantic Ocean but also features a number of large and important rivers.

The European explorers who came to the region in the 16th and 17th centuries were the first to refer to it as Guyana. The original Guyana was larger and was marked by the triangle formed by three major South American rivers—the Amazon, Negro, and Orinoco. The region included what today are the countries of Guyana, Suriname (formerly Dutch Guiana), and French Guiana, as well as part of Venezuela.

Present-day Guyana consists of 83,000 square miles (214,970 square kilometers), making it slightly smaller than the state of Idaho. It has a coastline along the Atlantic Ocean of 270 miles (435 km), which makes up the northern border of the country. Several rivers help make up Guyana's border on the west with Venezuela and Brazil. Brazil also lies to the south, separated from Guyana by the Akarai Mountains. The Courantyne River forms the country's eastern border with Suriname.

The three largest rivers in the country are the Berbice, Demerara, and Essequibo. One of Guyana's most notable landmarks is Kaieteur Falls, located on the Potaro River in west-central Guyana. There the water tumbles more than 740 feet (225 meters).

Some early European explorers believed that Guyana was the location of *El Dorado*, a mythical land filled with golden cities and great wealth. In truth, Guyana does produce gold and diamonds, though not nearly in the quantities the explorers were hoping for. *Bauxite*, which is used to make aluminum, is in fact the country's most abundant mineral.

Words to Understand in this Chapter

bauxite—a mineral that is used to make aluminum.
El Dorado—the mythical city of gold and diamonds that some believed was located in Guyana.
endangered—nearing extinction (as a wildlife species).
equatorial—located at or near the equator.
erosion—the gradual wearing away of a coastline into the sea.
savanna—a grassy plain with very few trees.

Floodwaters sweep through the rain forest in Guyana. The rain forest covers three-quarters of the country's land area.

Three Regions

The land of Guyana can be divided into three main ecological regions: a *savanna*, an *equatorial* rain forest, and a coastal plain.

The Rupununi Savannas, a region of grassy plains, lie in the far southwest portion of Guyana—the furthest region from the Atlantic Ocean. The flat, grassy land of the Rapununi Savannas is still used by some cattle ranchers. One mountainous area, the Kanuku Mountains, is part of this region. Native people farm some of the land at the foot of the mountain range.

The equatorial rain forest makes up more than three-fourths of the land area of Guyana. (A tropical rain forest is a woodland that receives at least 100 inches, or 254 centimeters, of rainfall annually.) It runs from the far south up

The white-faced Saki monkey lives in the rainforest of Guyana.

through the middle of the country and toward the ocean. The land in this area is made up of a mixture of sandy soil and clay, and it is home to most of the country's forest and mineral resources. Despite being a great source of wealth, the rain forest is still largely unsettled. The people who do live in this region are typically part of a lumber or mining camp. The western portion of this region is made up of the Pakaraima Mountains. This range includes the highest peak in Guyana, Mount Roraima, which reaches 9,219 feet (2,812 meters). The Potaro River runs east from this mountain range and includes the picturesque Kaieteur Falls, located in Kaieteur National Park.

The coastal plain is a narrow strip of land closest to the Atlantic Ocean, along the country's northern border. While this area measures just 10 to 40 miles (16 to 65 km) wide and makes up only about 7 percent of the landmass of the country, it is home to more than 90 percent of Guyana's population. In addition to having the capital city of Georgetown, this region also supports most of the agricultural industry in Guyana, including all of its sugar operations. *Erosion* of the coastline is a major concern, however, as the springtime pounding from the tide has caused some areas nearest the sea to fall below sea level. The Guyanese people's only means of protection against the tide is to build seawalls and dams.

Quick Facts: The Geography of Guyana

Location: Northern South America, bordering the Atlantic Ocean between Suriname and Venezuela

Area: (slightly smaller than Idaho)
  total: 83,000 square miles (214,970 sq km)
  land: 76,004 square miles (196,850 sq km)
  water: 6,996 square miles (18,120 sq km)

Borders: Brazil, 695 miles (1,119 km); Suriname, 238 miles (600 km); Venezuela, 462 miles (743 km)

Climate: tropical, hot, humid, moderated by northeast trade winds; two rainy seasons (May to mid-August, mid-November to mid-January)

Terrain: mostly rolling highlands, low coastal plain; savanna in the south

Elevation extremes:
  lowest point: Atlantic Ocean—0 feet
  highest point: Mount Roraima—9,219 feet (2,812 meters)

Natural hazards: flash floods are a constant threat during rainy seasons

Source: CIA World Factbook 2015.

Climate

Because of its location near the equator, Guyana's climate is tropical. Most of the year it is warm and humid with very little variation in temperature. In fact, the temperature varies more from daytime to nighttime than it does from season to season.

The coastline is affected by northeast trade winds, and its seaside location ensures that temperature changes rarely occur. This region has the mildest weather in Guyana, with average temperatures around 80°F (27°C). In the interior rain forest areas, however, temperatures can surpass 100°F (38°C) and are made even more uncomfortable by the high humidity com-

The endangered harpy eagle, which is native to the Guyanese rain forest, is the largest of all eagle species. It can grow to 2.8 feet (86 cm) long with a wingspan of more than 6 feet (2 meters).

mon to rain forests.

Guyana also receives a great deal of rainfall, especially along the coast. An average of 90 inches (229 cm) of rain falls in the Georgetown area, while the Rupununi Savannas receive about 60 inches (152 cm) per year. The rainiest time of the year is from the end of May through July in coastal areas and from April through September in the central part of the country. The hottest time of the year is from September through November, when rainfall is at its lowest.

Plants and Animals

Plant and animal life in Guyana varies by region. In the coastal plain, the damp, almost swampy conditions make a perfect home for marsh grasses and underwater vegetation. The rain forests are home to huge trees with long vines and rich vegetation. Some beautiful flowers such as orchids grow in this region as well. The Rupununi Savannas have mostly grassy areas.

The animal life of Guyana is also rich and varied. In the seawater along the coast, you can find the *endangered* manatee (known to some as "the gentle sea cow"), along with water-loving birds like ducks, herons, and kingfishers.

The rain forest also makes a great home for many varieties of wildlife, from the two-toed sloth to the capuchin monkey to a number of different types of lizards, frogs, and snakes. Various bird species, including colorful macaws, parrots, and parakeets and the imposing harpy eagle can also be found there. In the grassland areas, wildlife includes the peculiar-looking armadillo.

TEXT-DEPENDENT QUESTIONS

1. How high is the waterfall at Kaieteur Falls?
2. What is Guyana's most abundant mineral?
3. What mountain range is found in the Rupununi Savannas?

Historians believe that the Warau had been the first to live in the region, followed by the Arawaks. Both were peaceful tribes of hunter-gatherers and fishermen. The more aggressive Caribs arrived in the 14th century from central South America.

Early exploration of the area by the Spanish was less than fruitful. They had already discovered other lands that they deemed to be more plentiful in the mineral resources they sought. To the Spanish, Guyana and the surrounding area seemed unattractive in comparison.

That attitude toward Guyana changed briefly in the mid-16th century,

Words to Understand in this Chapter

apprenticeship—a period of time in which a worker learns a trade under supervision.

colony—an area of land that is ruled by a far-off country.

commune—a community in which possessions and responsibilities are shared.

communism—a form of government that advocates common ownership of the means of production and distribution of goods based on need.

expedition—a journey for a particular purpose, such as to discover or explore uncharted land.

exports—products that are manufactured or produced in one country but sold to a foreign country.

indenture—a contract that binds one person to work for another for a period of time.

plantations—large tracts of land where a single crop is typically grown; in the past, plantations were often worked by slaves.

polder—the Dutch system of water management, which uses dams and canals to control water in an agricultural area.

rebellion—an uprising against a government or authority by a group.

This 19th-century print shows a Warau house in Guyana. The Warau have lived on the northwest coast of Guyana for more than 7,000 years. Their development of the dugout canoe helped spread Warau culture through the region. Another group of Native Americans, the Arawak, moved into the Guyana region around 3,500 years ago.

when those searching for the mythical land of El Dorado concentrated on the Guyana area. El Dorado was believed to be a city of gold and diamonds, and a man named Pedro da Silva led an expedition of 2,000 soldiers and adventurers into the region in and around what today is Guyana. The effort proved fruitless, however, and only 50 of Silva's men are believed to have survived the expedition.

First Settlements

Although the Spanish were the earliest European explorers, they were not the first to settle in the Guyana area. In 1616 colonists from Holland established the first European settlement in the region. Their first goal was to trade with the native population. The first trading post was set up near the mouth of the Essequibo River. Soon, the Dutch had established other settlements in the area.

A map of the Americas by the Dutch cartographer Willem Blaeu, circa 1630. During the 17th century Holland competed with Spain, England, France, and Portugal to establish colonies in the New World.

The first Dutch *colony* was called Essequibo. It was managed by the Dutch West India Company, a group of investors sponsored by the government. A later colony was called Berbice. During this period, other European countries were also establishing colonies in both North and South America. The Dutch were eventually forced to defend their settlements in Guyana against the French and British, as well as against the Spanish, all of whom had established their own colonies in the region. In 1648 Spain and the Netherlands signed the Treaty of Münster in Münster, Germany, which recognized each other's possessions throughout the world. For all interested European powers, this treaty gave the Netherlands official control of Guyana.

The coastal lands of Guyana were the best for growing crops, but constant flooding in the area made farming difficult. The problems were not insurmountable, however. The Dutch settlers implemented their *polder* system, which they had already developed back in Holland. This system used a series of dams and canals to keep saltwater away from the croplands, and it managed the freshwater in the area for the benefit of the crops.

The Dutch soon began to develop sugar and tobacco *plantations* in the region, and their crops became valuable *exports*. But they required people to labor in the fields, and the natives did not suit their needs. The Dutch West India Company began to import African slaves to help work the land. By the 1660s, there were about 2,500 slaves in the region.

Deplorable conditions for the slaves led to a number of uprisings. The most notable occurred in 1763, when a slave named Cuffy led a *rebellion* on several plantations along the Canje River. European settlers were forced to flee their plantations. For nearly a year, the slaves maintained control of the land. Not until troops from neighboring French and British colonies arrived to assist the Dutch were the slaves defeated. Today, Cuffy is still revered as a hero in Guyana.

British Control

In 1746 the Dutch opened a settlement near the Demerara River to English people, many of whom quickly left their settlements in the islands of the Lesser Antilles for the more favorable growing conditions in Guyana. As the British population in the region increased, however, a battle for control commenced.

In 1781 the British took control of Dutch settlements and established Georgetown, which was named for King George III. The French took control in 1782, and the Dutch regained power from 1784 to 1796. The British took back the land by force in 1797, losing control to the Dutch again in 1803. Finally, at the London Convention of 1814, the area was formally unified under British rule as British Guiana.

The British preserved the Dutch polder system and were successful in growing crops and creating a viable economy for British Guiana. The health, education, and transportation systems also improved.

In 1834 slavery was abolished in all of the British colonies. Former slaves served a four-year paid *apprenticeship*, and in 1838 they were given complete freedom.

Once the slaves received their freedom, most elected to leave the plantations where they had been enslaved. This flight from the plantations created

Much of Guyana remains wilderness, as it was when the American naturalist William La Varre explored the jungle rivers in the 1930s.

a shortage of workers. To resolve the shortage, the British started an *indenture* system, under which immigrants were given free passage to British Guiana in exchange for a contract to work for a predetermined number of years. At the end of their work period, they could return to their homeland or choose to stay in British Guiana. For more than 100 years, workers came to British Guiana from China, East India, Africa, the West Indies, and even parts of Europe.

During this period, a representative of the British monarchy was head of government, but local authorities controlled all of British Guiana's financial matters. In 1928 a new constitution placed all power into the hands of the British crown.

Nationalism

It wasn't until 1950 that the people of British Guiana made a concerted effort to govern themselves. The People's Progressive Party (PPP), formed by Cheddi Berrat Jagan and Linden Forbes Burnham, was the country's first political party. The PPP was a conservative group. But in the view of some people—including the British government—the PPP leaned toward the beliefs of *communism*.

In 1953 a new constitution granted citizens the right to vote. After the first democratic elections left the PPP in control of the government, the British threw out the constitution and installed an interim government. In 1955 Burnham split off from the PPP and formed the People's National Congress, which quickly became a rival of the PPP. In 1957 new elections were held, and the PPP won most of the seats in the new legislature. Jagan became prime minister until 1964, when Burnham took over the position. On May 26, 1966, Guyana became an independent nation.

The Jonestown Tragedy

One of the most tragic events of the late 20th century took place in Guyana in 1978. Jonestown, an agricultural *commune* in northwestern Guyana, was home to a religious cult called the People's Temple. The leader of the cult was a man named Jim Jones. As Jones's group grew in number, rumors of his mistreatment of followers began to surface. These stories became worldwide news, and Jones fortified his settlement with armed guards, cutting his followers off from the outside world. In November 1978,

Cheddi Berrat Jagan (1918–1997) was the most important figure in Guyana's history during the 20th century. Born the son of indentured plantation workers from India, Jagan eventually attended college in the United States and became a dentist. In the 1940s, Jagan became active politically and fought for Guyana's independence from Great Britain. This was eventually accomplished in 1966. Elected president of Guyana in 1992, Jagan served in that office until his death. His wife, Janet, succeeded him.

California congressman Leo Ryan visited the encampment to investigate, whereupon he and other visitors were murdered. That same night, Jones commanded his followers to commit suicide by drinking poison. More than 900 people died.

The Presidency

A new constitution in 1980 added the office of president, which Linden Forbes Burnham won in 1981. Following Burnham's death in 1985, Desmond Hoyte took over the presidency, only to lose the 1992 election to Cheddi Jagan. Jagan died in office in 1997.

The bodies of some of the 912 people who died in a mass suicide in Jonestown. On November 17, 1978, People's Temple cult leader Jim Jones ordered his followers to drink poison and kill themselves.

Bharrat Jagdeo was elected president in 2001, and Samuel Hinds was elected prime minister the same year. Despite suspected mismanagement during his administration, Jagdeo was reelected in 2006. The election was deemed fair and open.

Donald Ramotar

In 2011, Donald Ramotar was elected president of Guyana. However, he won with less than a majority, receiving only 49% percent of vote, and his People's Progressive Party also received less than a majority in parliament, although it still held more seats than any other party. These facts have made it challenging to govern, and Guyana's economic problems have contributed to Ramotar's unpopularity. In November 2014, Ramotar's opponents, who constituted a majority in parliament, proposed holding a "no-confidence" vote. If the vote had passed, national elections for president would have been held more than a year early. To prevent this, Ramotar invoked an obscure constitutional provision that allowed him to suspend the parliamentary session for six months. Critics of the administration complained that Ramotar was subverting democracy in Guyana.

TEXT-DEPENDENT QUESTIONS
1. In what year did the British establish Georgetown?
2. What two Guyanese leaders formed the People's Progressive Party?

(Opposite) Produce displayed for sale at a market in Parika. (Right) A woman prepares *cachiri*, a popular drink, in a workshop near the border with Venezuela. Agriculture is an important part of Guyana's economy.

3 A Fragile Economy

GUYANA, ONE OF the poorest countries in the Western Hemisphere, faces a variety of economic challenges. Its economy is small and based on only a few key components such as sugar production and bauxite mining. Thus, declines in world prices for these commodities can, and have, hit Guyana hard. In addition, Guyana suffers from a shortage of skilled workers and a poor *infrastructure*. The country's foreign debt is large. Corruption is rampant.

On the plus side, Guyana undertook a program of economic reforms beginning in 1989. Previously, the nation's economy had been controlled by the government and suffered from massive inefficiencies. After moving toward a more open, free-market-oriented system, Guyana began to experience modest economic growth in the late 1990s. Still, significant problems remain.

In 2014, the World Bank estimated Guyana's gross domestic product (GDP) at about $5.5 billion. (GDP is the total value of all goods and services a nation produces annually.) That year, Guyana ranked as the world's 174th-largest economy. Each citizen's share of Guyana's annual economic activity stood at an estimated $6,900 in 2014, one of the lowest in South America.

Guyana's economy is heavily dependent upon the export of six commodities—sugar, gold, bauxite, shrimp, timber, and rice. Together, these represent nearly 60 percent of Guyana's gross domestic product. However, all are highly susceptible to adverse weather conditions, as well as fluctuations in commodity prices.

Despite resources such as fertile land for sugarcane fields and sizeable mineral deposits, Guyana is a desperately poor country. Some reports have placed unemployment at 11 percent, others as high as 25 percent.

During the 1970s and 1980s, Guyana borrowed heavily from foreign nations and financial agencies such as the World Bank and various international development funds. During the early 2000s, the government made an effort to begin reducing Guyana's debt. New policies, combined with the forgiveness of nearly $470 million in debt by the Inter-American Development

Words to Understand in this Chapter

emancipation—the end of the system of slavery.
infrastructure—the system of public works of a country or region, including roads, railways, bridges, and utilities.

Bank in 2007, have significantly reduced the amount of money the country pays in interest and principal each year, which has feed up more funds for economic development. Guyana's national debt is now about half of what it was in the early 1990s, but more work needs to be done to keep the country on a sustainable path.

Agriculture

Sugar is the number-one crop produced in Guyana, although its status within the country has always been somewhat tenuous due to water management concerns. The only land in the country suitable for sugar growing is along the coastal plain. The original Dutch system of water control has been effective, but it is also expensive to maintain.

Sugar operations gained a foothold during the era of slavery, which ended in 1834. During those years, roughly 80,000 slaves worked on about 400 sugar plantations. Following *emancipation*, many of the sugar plantations went out of business because the labor was no longer free. Consolidation of the remaining operations, however, allowed the industry to continue to thrive. Today, nearly half of the tax revenue received by the government comes from the sugar industry. According to some estimates, sugar-related work supports nearly 80 percent of the people of Guyana.

During 2014, production of sugar in Guyana dropped to a 24-year low. In response, during 2015 President Donald Ramotar proposed investing $96 million to upgrade facilities and build new processing plants. Part of his proposal included facilities for the production of ethanol, a biofuel that is used as an additive to gasoline.

The second-largest crop in Guyana is rice, but it is grown more for domestic purposes than for export. More than half of the rice grown in Guyana is consumed there. Citrus fruits, cocoa, and coconuts are also cultivated in the country.

Roughly 75 percent of the land in Guyana is forested, but the timber industry didn't begin to develop until the 1990s, when some Asian timber companies began logging in parts of the rain forest. Environmental groups and Guyana's native population have fought against the logging, but the

Prince Charles of Great Britain speaks with a Guyanese schoolgirl at Tagore Memorial School. Guyana has a strong system of education and a high literacy rate; 99 percent of people over age 15 have attended school.

Quick Facts: The Economy of Guyana

Gross domestic product (GDP*):
$5.498 billion
GDP per capita: $6,900
Natural resources: bauxite, gold, diamonds, hardwood timber, shrimp, fish.
Agriculture (20.3% of GDP): sugarcane, rice, edible oils; beef, pork, poultry; shrimp, fish.
Industry (39.2% of GDP): bauxite, sugar, rice milling, timber, textiles, gold mining.
Services (40.5% of GDP): finance, transportation, communication, schools, hospitals, government agencies, tourism.

Inflation: 2.5%
Foreign trade:
Exports—$1.308 billion: sugar, gold, bauxite, alumina, rice, shrimp, molasses, rum, timber.
Imports—$1.981 billion: manufactures, machinery, petroleum, food.
Currency exchange rate: 207.2 Guyanese dollars = US $1 (2015).

*Gross domestic product (GDP) represents the total value of goods and services produced in a country during a particular year.
All figures are 2014 estimates unless otherwise noted.
Source: CIA World Factbook 2015.

biggest hindrance to its development has been a lack of transportation options for the cut timber. Roads are underdeveloped, and it is difficult to float the logs down the rivers to developed areas.

Mining

Bauxite, which is used to make aluminum, is the second-largest source of income in Guyana. The country currently ranks among the world's top producers of bauxite, although the industry faces some difficulties due to rising fuel costs and international competition from countries such as China. Two companies control the industry, and there are two main operations for extracting the ore, one located on the Demerara River, the other on the

Berbice River. Bauxite exists beneath the layers of sand and clay, and workers remove the top layers to expose the bauxite. Much of the ore is shipped to the United States.

Since the late 19th century, gold and diamonds have been mined in Guyana. Much of Guyana's economic growth in recent years has come from a surge in gold production in response to global prices. However, downward trends in gold prices during 2014 and 2015 could have a negative effect on Guyana's economy.

One of Guyana's leading gold mines, the Omai mine, was the source of one of the country's worst industrial accidents. In 1995 the mine was responsible for the spillage of 3.5 million tons of water containing traces of the deadly compound cyanide into a tributary that leads into the Essequibo River. This environmental catastrophe caused the country's gold production to be temporarily shut down.

Bauxite is an ore that can be processed to make aluminum.

Other Factors

Manufacturing in Guyana revolves primarily around the other main industries in the country. For example, processing of sugar and bauxite are prime manufacturing operations. Processing plants for other crops, such as coconuts and rice, also operate in the country, as do mineral processing plants for gold and diamonds.

The service sector of Guyana includes the banking industry, transportation, and communications. The Bank of Guyana is the central bank, but other private operations also serve Guyanese bankers. Road transportation is underdeveloped in the country, mainly because the waterways are still a major avenue for people and goods to move from place to place. Guyana has fewer than 400 miles (590 km) of paved highway.

The communications system has been improving in recent years. In 2012 government statistics indicated that nearly 550,000 Guyanese owned cellular phones. Another 150,00 had telephone service in their homes, although many areas still lacked fixed-line telephone services. There are three television stations in Guyana: one owned by the government, and two private stations that carry programs from the United States via satellite. In 2012 it was estimated that there were 24,000 Internet hosts available in the country, and an estimated 190,000 people had Internet access.

 ## TEXT-DEPENDENT QUESTIONS

1. What is the number-one agricultural crop produced in Guyana?
2. What is the unemployment rate in Guyana?

(Opposite) A Guyanese girl wears a fringed dress and a variety of necklaces, circa 1955. (Right) Great Britain's Prince Charles attends a local dance. Because of the many peoples who have settled in Guyana, its culture is very diverse today.

4 Many Peoples, Diverse Culture

MORE THAN MOST societies in the region, the Guyanese people are a melting pot of different backgrounds. Slavery brought a large number of people from Africa, and following emancipation, the indenture system brought in people from a variety of other countries and cultures. These people brought with them their own religions, languages, and traditions, which together with the culture of the *indigenous* people have made Guyana a very diverse country. However, because such a large percentage of the country's land is not developed, Guyana has a small population: only about 735,000 people.

Guyana's emigration rate is among the highest in the world—more than 400,000 Guyanese have left the country and are living and working elsewhere in Latin America or the Caribbean. Money they send home to their families, known as remittances, are a vital source of income for many Guyanese families.

One key difference between Guyana and many of its Spanish- and French-speaking neighbors is its national language, English. Guyana is the only South American country in which English is the main language, and has close ties to the English-speaking countries of the Caribbean. Two East Indian languages, Hindi and Urdu, are also spoken, as are Portuguese and Chinese to some degree. The native South American Indians also speak their own languages.

Ethnic Groups

People of East Indian descent form the largest ethnic group in Guyana. Following emancipation of the African slaves in 1834, East Indians (people from Southeast Asia, particularly India, Indochina, and Malaysia) were the greatest participants in the recently established indenture system. Today, about 44 percent of the population of Guyana claims East Indian ancestry; most of these people work in the sugar and rice industries.

About 30 percent of Guyana's population is black, mostly descendants of African slaves. While their ancestors worked the plantations in the 17th,

Words to Understand in this Chapter

cricket—a sport similar to baseball that was introduced to Guyana by the British.
indigenous—growing or living naturally in a certain area.
literacy—the ability to read and write.
urbanized—taking on the qualities of a city environment.

18th, and 19th centuries, today's black population is more *urbanized*, centered in and around the capital city of Georgetown.

About 18 percent of Guyana's people are white, Chinese, or of mixed ancestry. Some in this group are descended from the original Dutch and British colonists, as well as the indentured servants who came from European countries such as Portugal.

Native Americans make up about 9 percent of the country's population.

Education

Unlike many poor countries, Guyana has a relatively strong system of education and a high *literacy* rate. The education system is funded by a partnership of private and public institutions. Most of the primary schools are

Although Guyana has been an independent nation since 1966, the country retains strong ties with Great Britain.

An American military doctor examines an elderly woman at a medical clinic for poor Guyanese that was set up in the library in the village of Mabaruma.

run by Christian churches, but many of the costs, including salaries for teachers and administrators, are paid for by the government.

Primary school runs for eight years, and according to the government all children in the country attend attend primary school. Among Guyanese age 15 and over, 85 percent can read and write. The Ramotar government has set a goal for all children to continue on to secondary school as well, although this has not yet been realized. President Ramotar has said that Guyana needs to develop a highly educated workforce in order to compete in the global economy. His critics have noted that although all Guyanese students are compelled to attend school, the value of the education they are receiving is often questionable. Two of the country's secondary schools are operated by the government, and the rest receive some government support. There is one national university, located in Georgetown, as well as some technical and trade schools.

According to some estimates, more than 80 percent of Guyanese citizens with college-level educations have emigrated to find jobs elsewhere. This brain drain has a serious effect on Guyana's industry, education, and health care systems. Guyana has one of the highest rates of HIV infection in South America, and must rely on international support for doctors and medical care.

Arts, Festivals, and Religion

Many of the cultural differences of the people who immigrated to Guyana have been preserved in the country's arts and culture. Guyanese artwork, music, and dance shows influences from African, East Indian, and Native American cultures.

Guyana's national dance company has a distinct East Indian flair. Artwork features many South American Indian traits, highlighting the beauty of the rain forest and the other natural resources of the land. Many of the festivals and celebrations have been shaped by African culture.

Religion is important to the people of Guyana, and many of the festivals and celebrations that take place throughout the year have a religious foundation. About a third of the population practices Hinduism, and about 7 percent are Muslims. Christians make up more than 50 percent of the popula-

The Hindu festival of Divali is popular in Guyana.

Quick Facts: The People of Guyana

Population: 735,554

Ethnic groups: East Indian 43.5%, black (African) 30.2%, mixed 16.7%, Amerindian 9.1%, other 0.5% (includes Portuguese, Chinese, white) (2002).

Age structure:
0–4 years: 29%
15–64 years: 63.5%
65 years and over: 7.5%

Population growth rate: -0.11%

Birth rate: 15.9 births/1,000 population

Death rate: 7.3 deaths/1,000 population

Infant mortality rate: 33.56 deaths/1,000 live births

Life expectancy at birth: 67.81 years

Total fertility rate: 2.14 children born/woman

Religions: Protestant 30.5%, Hindu 28.4%, Roman Catholic 8.1%, Muslim 7.2%, Jehovah's Witnesses 1.1%, other Christian 17.7%, other 1.9%, none 4.3%, unspecified 0.9% (2002).

Languages: English (official), Guyanese Creole, Amerindian languages (including Caribbean and Arawak languages), Indian languages (including Caribbean Hindustani, a dialect of Hindi), Chinese.

Literacy (age 15 and older): 85% (2009).

All figures are 2014 estimates unless otherwise noted.
Source: CIA World Factbook 2014.

tion, and the Christian celebrations of Lent and Christmas are widely observed each year.

Hindu people celebrate a festival of lights called Divali; they adorn their homes with special tiny lights for the occasion. In June, the Muslim festival of Yum an-Nabi, which celebrates the birth of the prophet Muhammad, is observed.

Mashramani, which means "celebration of a job well done," is Guyana's Republic Day, a national holiday observed on February 23. Republic Day is marked by a week of special programs on television, celebrations in schools, and parades in the streets. Guyana also celebrates Independence Day on May 26 and Emancipation Day on August 1. Emancipation Day commemorates the end of slavery in 1834. On that day, the Parliament Building holds a celebration, and a number of other festivals take place throughout the country.

Recreation

While soccer is the most popular sport in much of Latin America, the national sport in Guyana is *cricket*, which is somewhat like baseball. Cricket, which is played by both men and women in Guyana, originated in England. The British brought the sport to Guyana during colonial times. Today, however, some Guyanese cricketers are so accomplished at the sport that they are recruited to go to England to play for cricket clubs there. In 2007, Providence Stadium opened in Georgetown to host cricket matches, becoming Guyana's largest sports complex by far.

Volleyball and soccer are also very popular in Guyana. Other sports played there include basketball, tennis, golf, badminton, field hockey, and even American football.

Dominoes is a national passion in Guyana. Men and women often can be seen playing the table game at social gatherings. There are also organized dominoes tournaments throughout the country.

 TEXT-DEPENDENT QUESTIONS

1. What distinguishes Guyana from many of its neighbors?
2. What is the largest ethnic group in Guyana?

(Opposite) St. George's Anglican Cathedral in Georgetown, built in 1899, is one of the tallest wooden churches in the world. (Right) A painting of a British settlement in Guyana, circa 1834. Today, the country's largest city is Georgetown.

5 Guyana's Communities

GUYANA HAS ONE of the lowest *population densities* of any country in Latin America. This is due in large part to the terrain: a very small percentage of the land is habitable for large numbers of people. The rain forest and rough terrain also make movement from one part of the country to another difficult.

Because of the terrain, about 90 percent of the Guyanese population lives in the northern part of the country, most of them along the coastal plain and near the point where a major river empties into the Atlantic Ocean. Despite the rich resources available in the country's interior, the land is mostly devoid of humans except for small mining and timber camps.

Guyana has only one city that can be classified as a truly urban center—

the capital city of Georgetown. Its population of about 235,000 is more than one-fourth of the population of the entire country. Even along the coastal plain, where most of the population lives, about 70 percent of the region is considered rural.

Georgetown

Named for England's King George III, the capital city is more than 200 years old. It is located on the east bank of the Demerara River and serves as the country's center of commerce and shipping activity. Most of the country's exports of sugar, bauxite, and other crops and minerals leave through ports in Georgetown.

To someone looking from the air, Georgetown would appear much like many cities its size in the world, with streets laid out in a *grid* pattern and lined with houses. But a closer look reveals the effects of its low elevation and close proximity to the sea. Many streets have canals running through them, and most of the houses are raised off the ground on stilts or bricks in order to prevent damage from flooding.

Words to Understand in this Chapter

grid—a framework in which spaces (such as streets) are parallel to, or cross, each other.
population density—the number of people living per unit of an area (for example, a square mile or square kilometer).

Guyana's interior remains forested and undeveloped, and most of its people live along the coastal plain.

Much of the business activity is centered near the waterfront areas, while the government offices are located closer to the city's center.

Other Towns

There are only five other towns in Guyana that are large and organized enough to have their own city governments. Two important cities are Linden and New Amsterdam. Linden, located on the Demerara River about 66 miles (106 km) from Georgetown, is a mining town with a population of about

Guyana's parliament meets in this building in Georgetown.

45,000, making it the second-largest city in Guyana. It is the farthest from the ocean of any of the bigger towns.

New Amsterdam, located on the east bank of the Berbice River, is the capital of the East Berbice-Corentyne region. The home of much of the bauxite export business, New Amsterdam has a population of about 35,000.

Corriverton, located at the mouth of the Courantyne River, has a small port that serves passengers heading to nearby Suriname. Its population is less than 12,000.

Other Guyanese towns with more than 3,000 inhabitants include Bartica, Skeldon, Rosignol, Mahaica, Mahdia, Kumaka, Paradise, and Vreed en Hoop.

Rural life

Even along the coastal plain, much of the land is rural, consisting of plantations and small farming villages along the coastline and riverbanks. These villages may hold a couple thousand people, but most are home to only a few hundred.

Quick Facts: Guyana's Largest Cities and Towns

		Population			Population
1.	Georgetown	235,017	6. Bartica		11,157
2.	Linden	44,690	7. Skeldon		5,859
3.	New Amsterdam	35,039	8. Rosignol		5,782
4.	Anna Regina	12,448	9. Mahaica		4,867
5.	Corriverton	11,536	10. Mahdia		4,200

Figures are 2015 estimates. Source: Guyanese Institute of Geography and Statistics

The interior of the country is where the South American Indians make their home. While they represent a very small percentage of the overall population of Guyana, these indigenous people make up the majority of the population outside the coastal plain. They live much as their ancestors did, surviving off their own abilities as hunters, fishermen, and farmers.

TEXT-DEPENDENT QUESTIONS

1. What is the population density of Guyana?
2. On what river is Georgetown, the capital of Guyana, located?
3. What is the second-largest city in Guyana?

The religious freedom guaranteed by Guyana's constitution is reflected in the country's national celebrations. Guyana has large groups of Christians, Hindus, and Muslims, and all the major religious holidays celebrated by the three faiths are observed nationally.

January

Guyanese Christians welcome **New Year's Day** by attending midnight Mass; others go to big parties either in private homes or in public places.

February

Republic Day, or Mashramani, celebrates the day in 1970 when Guyana declared itself a s overeign democratic republic and severed its ties to the British crown. This national holiday takes place on February 23. During the week before Republic Day, the country hosts competitions for calypso, steel, and masquerade bands as well as sports activities and competitions for children. A "Miss Mash" is picked from the winners of each of the regional beauty pageants. At midnight on February 22, flag-raising ceremonies are held throughout Guyana and the president of Guyana addresses the country. On Republic Day, the people celebrate with parades and music in a carnival-like atmosphere.

March

The Hindu festival of **Phagwa** is celebrated in March during the full moon. The event celebrates spring and the triumph of good over evil.

Preparation for Phagwa begins weeks in advance as singing groups assemble to sing religious songs at temples and homes. On the morning of Phagwa, Hindus attend services and offer special prayers of thanks. Later, they share food and everyone sings and dances. In addition, perfume, powder, red dye, and water are sprinkled on the celebrants.

April

The Christian feast days of **Good Friday** and **Easter** take place in March or April (the dates vary from year to year). Many attend church ceremonies, and children receive gifts of candy and Easter eggs. Among Guyana's traditional Easter weekend events are kite-flying, picnics, and the **Bartica Regatta**, which includes all kinds of swimming activities and powerboat races.

May

On May 1, the Guyanese celebrate **Labour Day**, which recognizes workers around the world. In Georgetown, workers parade around the city carrying banners and wearing red shirts to represent their struggles. A huge rally is held at the National Park in Thomas Lands and features speeches by the president of the Trade Union Congress, other trade officials, and sometimes even the president of the country.

Guyana's independently administered constitution went into effect May 26, 1966, and the Guyanese people now celebrate this day as **Independence Day**. The national flag is raised throughout the country at midnight on May 25.

The president of Guyana addresses the nation after a fireworks display. Guyana's national awards—the Orders of Guyana—usually are announced on Independence Day.

June

The Muslim festival of **Yum an-Nabi** celebrates the birthday of the prophet Muhammad, but it is held on various days in June. Muslims congregate for special services and listen to readings and teachings about Muhammad and the way he lived his life.

July

CARICOM Day, the first Monday in July, recognizes the Caribbean Community and Common Market (CARICOM). This special day includes official gatherings and political messages from those who are members of the group.

August

Emancipation Day, August 1, commemorates the abolition of slavery in 1834. On the day before Emancipation Day, the Parliament Building holds a liberation ceremony. On August 1, a folk festival graces National Park. Many communities hold their own celebrations as well.

October/November

Divali, the "Festival of Lights," is celebrated in the Hindu month of Kartik. Every Hindu home lights tiny lamps, and religious services are held throughout the country. Several communities hold motorcades that meet in central locations to celebrate. In Georgetown, a fashion parade finds young women competing for the title of Miss Diwali.

December

Christians in Guyana celebrate **Christmas**, the birthday of Jesus Christ, on December 25. Preparation beings early in December with people readying their homes for company. They prepare special foods and hang decorations. Many Guyanese attend midnight Mass on Christmas Eve. Family members gather for lunch Christmas Day and exchange gifts.

Boxing Day, December 26, is a time for friends and family to gather while finding entertainment from colorful masquerade bands who parade through the streets playing flutes and drums. Mother Sally, a person dressed as a doll on stilts, entertains everyone by dancing.

 **Recipes**

Cassava Puffs
1 pound cassava
1 egg
2 tbsp margarine
White pepper and salt to taste
1 tsp baking powder
Oil for frying

Directions:
1. Boil the cassava, and while hot, crush until smooth.
2. Add lightly beaten egg, margarine, pepper, salt, and baking powder. Mix thoroughly.
3. Form into small balls and coat with flour. Fry in hot oil until brown.
4. Drain and serve.

Coo-Coo
4 to 6 medium-sized ochroes
2 cups water
1 tsp salt
1 cup cornmeal
1 tbsp butter or margarine
1 piece of cooked salt beef

Directions:
1. Slice the ochroes. Cut the salt beef into small pieces, add sliced ochroes and 1 cup of water, and cook until soft. Stir.
2. Mix the cornmeal with 1 cup of cold water and stir into a boiling liquid.
3. Cook until thick and smooth, beating all the time. If desired, turn into a greased mold.

Yam Foo-Foo
2 pounds hard yams
1 pound cassava

Directions:
1. Wash, peel, and boil the vegetables until tender. When cooked, leave in boiling water.
2. Remove the central fibrous string from the cassava, and pound the cassava and yams separately.
3. Combine the mashed cassava and yams, and pound to a fine texture until completely mixed. It should be smooth and firm, but not too stiff.
4. Dip a spoon in clean, warm water and remove the foo-foo in "balls."
5. Cover and keep warm, serving in soup.

Pineapple Tarts

2 cans crushed pineapple
Sugar (to taste)
1 large egg
16 oz flour
8 oz shortening

Directions:

1. Drain most of the liquid from the pineapple in the cans, then empty the cans into a pot. Add sugar until the sweetness is to your liking.
2. Boil the pineapple on medium heat until the juice is absorbed but the fruit is not dry. Stir often to avoid burning. Put aside to cool.
3. Prepare the pastry by mixing the flour and shortening together until the mixture becomes crumbly like bread crumbs.
4. Then, as you mix with your hands, add small amounts of ice-cold water as needed, and knead until the flour mixture becomes soft and doughy.
5. Break off one-inch balls and roll out into thin rounds.
6. Put some of the pineapple mixture in the center of each round, then close the pastry over the filling to form a triangle-shaped tart. Use a fork to pinch the corners shut.
7. Beat the egg in a bowl and brush it on top of the pineapple tarts.
8. Put the tarts in an oven preheated to 350°F and bake for 20–25 minutes or until done.

Plantain Chips

1 large green plantain (about 1 pound)
Vegetable oil
Salt

Directions:

1. Fill a deep fryer or large, heavy saucepan with vegetable oil to a depth of 2 to 3 inches and heat to about 375°F.
2. With a paring knife, trim off the ends of the plantain and cut in half crosswise. Make four slits lengthwise in the skin of the plantain halves, taking care not to slice the banana-like flesh inside. Use your fingers to pull off the skin.
3. Slice the plantain crosswise or diagonally into paper-thin rounds.
4. Deep-fry the plantain slices a dozen or so at a time, frying for 3 to 4 minutes and turning them until golden brown on both sides.
5. Take them out of the oil and place on a plate lined with brown paper to drain the oil.
6. When all the chips are fried, sprinkle them lightly with salt and serve.

Series Glossary

Amerindian—a term for the indigenous peoples of North, Central, and South America before the arrival of Europeans in the late 15th century.

Carnival—a popular festival in many South American countries, characterized by parades, dancing, and ornate costumes. It is celebrated just before the start of the Roman Catholic season of Lent, the 40-day period before Easter Sunday.

civil liberty—the right of people to do or say things that are not illegal without being stopped or interrupted by the government.

Communism—a political system in which all resources, industries, and property are considered to be held in common by all the people, with government as the central authority responsible for controlling all economic and social activity.

coup d'état—the violent overthrow of an existing government by a small group.

criollo—a resident of Spain's New World colonies who was born in North America to parents of Spanish ancestry. During the colonial period, criollos ranked above mestizos in the social order.

deforestation—the action or process of clearing forests.

economic system—the production, distribution, and consumption of goods and services within a country.

embargo—a government restriction or restraint on commerce, especially an order that prohibits trade with a particular nation.

foreign aid—financial assistance given by one country to another.

free trade—trade based on the unrestricted exchange of goods, with tariffs (taxes) only used to create revenue, not keep out foreign goods.

indigenous people—a name for native Amerindian tribes that lived in an area before Europeans came to settle there.

Latin America—a term for the areas of the American continents in which Spanish or Portuguese are the main languages. It includes nearly all of the Americas, except Canada, the United States, and a few small countries like Suriname and Guyana.

mestizo—a person of mixed Amerindian and European (typically Spanish) descent.

plaza—the central open square at the center of colonial-era cities in Latin America.

plebiscite—a vote by which the people of an entire country express their opinion on a particular government or national policy.

population density—a measurement of the number of people living in a specific area, such a square mile or square kilometer.

pre-Columbian—referring to a time before the 1490s, when Christopher Columbus landed in the Americas.

regime—a period of rule by a particular government, especially one that is considered to be oppressive.

Roman Catholicism—a Christian religion in which adherents obey the dictates of the Pope, whose headquarters is the Vatican in Rome. Roman Catholicism is the world's largest Christian denomination, with more than 1.2 billion members worldwide. Nearly 40 percent of Catholics live in Latin America.

service industry—any business, organization, or profession that does work for a customer, but is not involved in manufacturing.

Make Your Own Windmill

The trade winds play an important part in the weather in Guyana. Experiment with the wind in your own environment by creating your own windmill. The supplies you will need include a wooden dowel, one cardboard tube from a used paper towel roll, one push tack or a small nail, thread or light string, and tape.

1. Cut the cardboard tube lengthwise into four equal parts. Tape two of the cardboard strips together into the shape of a plus sign. Cut each end to a particularly rounded point. Be sure to keep the cuts equal and going in the same direction. This will allow your windmill to spin in one direction.
2. Tack or nail the windmill to the end of your dowel.
3. Once you've completed your windmill, try putting it in different areas outside to see where the wind is strongest. Experiment with taking your windmill outside at different times during the day and note when the wind is strongest.

Make Your Own Globe

Learn about Guyana's place in the world by making a papier-mâché globe of the Earth. Make the globe from a balloon covered with newspaper, flour-water glue, and paint.

1. Create a simple, thin glue by mixing one cup of water and one cup of flour until the mixture is thin and runny.
2. Have an adult stir the mixture into four cups of boiling water.
3. Simmer for about three minutes and then let it cool. Meanwhile, you can tear many strips of newspaper, about one-inch wide. The length isn't important.
4. Set these strips aside and blow up and tie a round balloon.
5. After the glue is cooled, dip each strip of paper in the flour glue, wipe off the excess, and wrap the strip around the balloon. Have at least three layers surrounding the balloon, but let each layer dry at least overnight before starting the next one.
6. After the last layer is placed on the balloon, let it dry thoroughly (it may take a few days). When the papier-mâché is dry, the balloon usually pops by itself and separates from the papier-mâché skin.
7. Using a globe or map of the Earth as your guide, draw the continents on the globe. Using tempera paint, paint the seven continents green.
8. When the continents are dry, paint the oceans blue.
9. Using a different color of your choice, paint the area that represents Guyana and the area where you live to see where you are located in relation to Guyana.

Project and Report Ideas

Flashcards

1. Make flashcards using the glossary terms in this book. Put the word on one side and the definition on the other.
2. In pairs, take turns saying the word and giving the definition.
3. Mix things up by giving the definition and having to come up with the glossary term. See how many you can get right in a row.

Ocean Life

Guyana borders the ocean, and fish are an important part of its people's diet. Learn more about the aquatic life off Guyana's shores by creating your own ocean diorama. A shoe box will serve as the stage containing your ocean scene.

1. Decorate the inside of the shoe box to look like it is underwater. Draw the ocean floor, water, rocks, coral, and seaweed—whatever you think you'd find in the waters near Guyana. If you like, you can find actual rocks and coral, and make "seaweed" by cutting out green construction paper in squiggly strips.
2. Find pictures of water animals that live in the area in old magazines or print them off the Internet. Cut them out and paste them on cardboard. Hang the creatures in your box using tape and thread.
3. Tape your seaweed and coral (if available) to the bottom of the box. Green and brown pipe cleaners make nice plants.

Cross-Curricular Reports

1. Surf the Internet and find websites related to Guyana. Choose the most interesting one and compile a list your class can put on its own Web page for other to use. Be sure to write one or two sentences about each website so people know what to expect of the site when they go there.
2. Write a one-page report about any of the following that interest you:
    - A particular animal found in Guyana—Describe what the animal looks like, where it can be found, what it eats, and other details you find interesting.
    - Bauxite—What is it and what is it used for?
    - Plantains—What are they and how do they grow? What nutrients do they offer and why are these nutrients important to a person's health?
    - The Guyanese savannas—What is a savanna? What types of plants and animals live in savannas?

Chronology

pre-1498	Arawak, Carib, and Warau Indians inhabit the land that is now Guyana.
1498	Christopher Columbus's third expedition sails past Guyana, becoming the first Europeans to see the land.
1593	Searching for the mythical city El Dorado, Pedro da Silva leads 2,000 explorers into Guyana; only about 50 survive.
1616	The Dutch establish the first European settlement in Guyana.
1621	The Dutch West India Company is given control of the region known as Essequibo.
1648	The Treaty of Münster gives the Dutch sovereign control of Guyana.
1660s	The Dutch West India Company begins to bring African slaves to Guyana to work on plantations.
1763	A slave named Cuffy leads a slave rebellion that forces many Europeans off the land for nearly a year.
1781–1813	The land of Guyana changes hands many times between the Dutch, British, and French.
1814	The country is formally unified under British rule as British Guiana at the London Convention.
1834	Slavery is abolished and the indenture system begins.
1879	Gold is discovered in Guyana.
1950	The People's Progressive Party is formed as the first political party in Guyana.
1953	After democratic elections put the PPP in power, Great Britain suspends Guiana's constitution and installs an interim government.
1957	The constitution is restored, and PPP leader Cheddi Jagan becomes prime minister.

1964	Linden Forbes Burnham, a PPP founder who split from Jagan to form the People's National Congress, takes power.
1966	Guyana becomes an independent nation on May 26.
1978	Members of the People's Temple religious cult commit suicide at the direction of their leader, Jim Jones.
1980	A new constitution creates the office of president, which Burnham wins the following year.
1992	Jagan wins the presidency.
1997	Jagan dies in office and is replaced by his wife, Janet.
1999	Bharrat Jagdeo becomes president.
2004	Workers and trade unions protest the European Union's decision to lower the price it will pay for Guyanese sugar.
2005	Over 30 people are killed and thousands left homeless in widespread flooding along Guyana's coast.
2006	An outbreak of gun violence prior to the presidential election kills several people, including Guyana's Agriculture Minister; Jagdeo is reelected president.
2007	A United Nations tribunal settles a territory dispute between Guyana and neighboring Suriname by giving both countries access to an offshore, potentially oil-rich area.
2010	Prolonged drought conditions harm the rice and sugar industries.
2011	In November, Donald Ramotar is elected president.
2016	Elections are scheduled for May.

Further Reading / Internet Resources

Ali, Arif. Guyana. Hertford, UK: Hansib Publishing, 2008.

Chasteen, John Charles. *Born in Blood and Fire: A Concise History of Latin America*. New York: W.W. Norton, 2011.

Keen, Benjamin, and Keith Haynes. *A History of Latin America.* Boston: Wadsworth Cengage Learning, 2013.

Smock, Kirk. *Guyana*. Guilford, Conn.: Bradt Travel Guides, 2008.

Stephenson, Denice, ed. *Dear People: Remembering Jonestown*. Berkeley, Calif.: Heyday Books, 2005.

Travel Information

http://www.geographia.com/guyana
http://www.state.gov/r/pa/ei/bgn/1984.htm
http://www.caribcentral.com/guyana/guytravel.htm

History and Geography

http://www.guyana.org/history.html
http://www.historycentral.com/NationbyNation/Guyana/History1.html

Economic and Political Information

http://www.gksoft.com/govt/en/gy.html
http://www.politicalresources.net/guyana.htm
https://www.cia.gov/llibrary/publications/the-world-factbook/geos/gy.html

Culture and Festivals

http://www.guyana.org/Handbook/festival.html
http://www.lonelyplanet.com/the-guianas/guyana

Caribbean/Latin American Action
1625 K Street NW, Suite 200
Washington, DC 20006
Phone: (202) 464-2031
Website: www.c-caa.org

Embassy of Guyana
2490 Tracy Place NW
Washington, D.C. 20008
Phone: (202) 265-6900
Fax: (202) 232-1297
Website: www.guyana.org
Email: guyanaembassydc@verizon.net

U.S. Agency for International Development
Ronald Reagan Building
Washington, D.C. 20523-0001
Phone: (202) 712-0000
Website: www.usaid.gov
Email: pinquiries@usaid.gov

U.S. Department of Commerce
International Trade Administration
Office of Latin America and the Caribbean
1401 Constitution Ave., NW
Washington, D.C. 20230
Phone: (202) 482-2000
Fax: (202) 482-5168
Website: www.commerce.gov
Email: publicaffairs@doc.gov

Index

Contributors

Senior Consulting Editor **James D. Henderson** is professor of international studies at Coastal Carolina University. He is the author of *Conservative Thought in Twentieth Century Latin America: The Ideals of Laureano Gómez* (1988; Spanish edition *Las ideas de Laureano Gómez* published in 1985); *When Colombia Bled: A History of the Violence in Tolima* (1985; Spanish edition *Cuando Colombia se desangró, una historia de la Violencia en metrópoli y provincia*, 1984); and coauthor of *A Reference Guide to Latin American History* (2000) and *Ten Notable Women of Latin America* (1978).

Mr. Henderson earned a bachelor's degree in history from Centenary College of Louisiana, and a master's degree in history from the University of Arizona. He then spent three years in the Peace Corps, serving in Colombia, before earning his doctorate in Latin American history in 1972 at Texas Christian University.

Bob Temple is the president of Red Line Editorial, Inc., an editorial services firm based in the Minneapolis-St. Paul area. Bob is an award-winning journalist who has enjoyed a 16-year career in newspapers and online journalism. He is the author of more than 20 nonfiction books for children and young adults, and seven Internet-related titles.